About the Author

Laura Hawryluck received her MD from the University of Western Ontario where she served her internal medicine residency. She completed a Fellowship in Critical Care at the University of Manitoba and MSc. in Bioethics from the University of Toronto, Canada. As a Professor of Critical Care Medicine at the University of Toronto, she was awarded the Queen's Golden Jubilee Medal for contributions to Canada in improving end-of-life care, the Medico-Legal Society of Toronto Award for contributions to medicine and law, and the University of Toronto Interdepartmental Critical Care Medicine Humanitarian Award for her contributions to international humanitarian work. She is the author of three other poetry books *An ICU Doctor's Reflections*, *Words that Matter* and *ICU Pandemic Diary* published by Olympia Publishers.

Our Stories

Dr. Laura A. Hawryluck

Our Stories

Olympia Publishers
London

www.olympiapublishers.com
OLYMPIA PAPERBACK EDITION

Copyright © Dr. Laura A. Hawryluck 2024

The right of Dr. Laura A. Hawryluck to be identified as author of this work has been asserted in accordance with sections 77 and 78 of the Copyright, Designs and Patents Act 1988.

All Rights Reserved

No reproduction, copy or transmission of this publication may be made without written permission. No paragraph of this publication may be reproduced, copied or transmitted save with the written permission of the publisher, or in accordance with the provisions of the Copyright Act 1956 (as amended).

Any person who commits any unauthorised act in relation to this publication may be liable to criminal prosecution and civil claims for damage.

A CIP catalogue record for this title is available from the British Library.

ISBN: 978-1-83543-118-4

This is a work of fiction.
Names, characters, places and incidents originate from the writer's imagination. Any resemblance to actual persons, living or dead, is purely coincidental.

First Published in 2024

Olympia Publishers
Tallis House
2 Tallis Street
London
EC4Y 0AB

Printed in Great Britain

Dedication

For Mary

Through faces rubbed raw with sorrow
From fields tilled, broken, and fallow,
    Joy raises her face to the light;
      Her arms worn ragged,
    Dripping debris and soil arid,
      Lift to the sky;
    And dreams take flight.

Acknowledgments

I want to thank everyone at Olympia for making this work a reality.

Every Morning

Every morning, the world comes undone.
Every morning, its songs are unsung.
Every morning, I stitch up the scars
From the wounds that mar.
Every morning, they break open
As though a terrible storm has spoken.
Though my stitches are stolen,
Hope remains my slogan.

Born

Words heard
Part of a line.
A spark captured in the mind
Turned over and over
Examined for its find.

What is the nature of such words?
Their draw
The tiniest threads of thought
That gnaw.
Both individual and collective,
Both annoying and reflective.

In loops spinning,
Fashioning a new beginning;
Desperate to make sense of troubles, emotions, life;
Desperate for acceptance;
A quest for sustenance;
Useless to even try to stop their imprinting;
Cut to the core—with a knife.

Yet, with enough depth of ideas,
Its plea is
See the many layers
Of what truth may be;
See the many layers
Of what may be me.

From an act of mind, a page torn;
From moments joyous, from moments forlorn,
A poem is born.

Crystal Light

Lights dancing on the tips of trees
Diamonds shifting in the breeze.
In the crystal light of morn,
So many daggers form.

Minds flicker,
Hearts whisper,
To live as all glitters;
To live as red and gold shimmers.

The Children of the Park

Sounds break the silence of the park;
When, like birds in spring,
Out, the joy of children playing rings;
Gone, the distance that keeps us apart.

Writing their names and messages in the mud;
Jumping and landing with satisfying thuds;
Soaring on swings;
Gliding down slides, laughing;
Climbing monkey bars and trees;
Scraping knees.

Even total blunders
Bring awe, new wonders.
What was once unknown
Now must be repeatedly shown.

With squeals of delight,
Running through sunlight,
Paper boats that sink too quick,
Games with sticks.
Blankets spread for family picnics.

Throughout the mix, see
Wagging tails chasing Frisbees.
Joyful barks
Echoing through the park.

Happiness transcends
As dusk descends.
And as darkness falls in the park,
And all, once again, depart,
Tales of the day fade into the dark.

Can you still look with a child's eyes
At life as sunny skies,
With the open heart
Of those magical days in the park?

Ukraine

All is calm and oh so bright
Snow has come to this December night.
Every branch outlined,
Every spike of every pine.

Pure and bright
Peace this night.
See how it glistens;
See how people listen.

Is peace at hand
As snow envelops this land?
Sweeps in the gaping holes in bedrooms and kitchens.
Crumpled buildings now snowcapped mountains;
As in the wind, curtains twitch out, twitch in
Some truths can't be hidden.

In the silence of sirens' screams,
Defense drones' intersections
Shivers and introspections.
Light far from serene.

The end of dreams
See the snow
Fiery, aglow.

More buildings crumble;
Toddlers frantically pulled from rubble;
And still, it snows,
Burying sorrows far below.

Cold and night.
Where, oh, where is it calm and bright?
Another playground massively torn;
Another child of war born.

A Canadian History

When the lights of the world go out
It's usually quietly,
Without a shout.
The people who care,
Not there;
Silenced deliberately
By others reveling in their own celebrity.
And in the terrible loss of innocence,
No voices with power to look askance.
Some turning a blind eye,
Living a lie;
Others not aware
Of future truths to be laid bare.

For a nation built at such a cost
The smiles of such precious children lost.
Hurt, horrific pain;
Disappearances unexplained;
Stained;
Forever shamed.

The children no longer there
Ripped from those who cared.
Then… silence that nothing can mend.
Trust at an absolute end.

By God,
(Is there really any God?)
Tell me, how do we heal?
Their stories are now mere lights strafed across fields.
When so much light has died
Gone, the future in our eyes.

Why do we let the lights go out?
Who lets light die?
Every day, we don't dare
To care.
It's you and I.

Two Girls

Two little girls out on the dock.
One who has;
One who has not.
Both at the same time spot a rock.

Has Not quicker with a stick
Snatched it up quick.
Has, all the while, leaned in slick.

One side rough and ragged,
Visible fault lines
Yet jagged edges still climb.

The other worn smooth by time,
Worn smooth by slime;
Unadorned.
Conformed.

The smooth is just like me.
Like you will one day be.
Worn by time,
Without a spine.
I don't have the luxury to be
Free.
To show my flaws

And where I have claws.
Conformed.
Unadorned.

Yet, with a quick flip
Of perception,
An honest slip
Of convention.

Peaks and valleys glint.
Sparkles fly across flint.
Beauty now explored.
Smooth now ignored.

A Bear

When I was young, I took you everywhere.
With you at my side, there was nothing I couldn't dare.
And as I held you close in the dark of night,
No one, nothing at all, could give me fright.

Throughout those young years,
Throughout the joys and tears,
You were loved with so much care,
Clearly seen in all your wear and tear,
Peering anxiously over your every repair.

I started to leave you behind,
Developed interests and friends of another kind.
Throughout all those years,
Throughout the failures, betrayals and tears,
Still weathered and worn
And repaired where you were torn.
You were always there,
Happily squeezed for hours without any other care.

And as I hold you close in the dark of days
When no one else knows what to say,
Through moments of fright
And endless nights,
I know I will find a way.

For the power of a bear is such,
Brimming with peace, loyalty and love,
Connected to the invincible child that once was.

A Heart So Deep

A heart that feels so deep,
Given to you in trust to keep.
Through moments of heartbreak,
So many times, more than you can take.
Seeing beauty everywhere
When so many don't even stop to care.

A heart that sees so deep,
Given to you in trust to keep.
Through moments of despair,
So many times, more than you can bear.
Witnessing everywhere moments of grace
When so many don't even slow their pace.

A heart that is touched so deep,
Given to you in trust to keep.
Through moments of intensity of feeling,
So many times, more than you can be concealing.
Finding tears pouring down your face
When so many don't even have wounds to erase.

A heart that hopes so deep,
Given to you in trust to keep.
Trying to see kindness' conquest
When so many don't even believe it exists.

Sentinel

In the light's morn',
Evergreen sentinels emerge from the mist.
Towering above the rocks, clenched like fists;
Softened by mischievous spring greens,
No one hears their screams.

Enveloping ghosts forlorn;
Memories of times of yore;
Memories of times before.

In the lake's borne,
Trunks gleaming in the light,
Haunting, pearly white,
Ghostly sentinels arch to the sky,
Defying any questions of why.
Roots arc still around stone,
Branches silenced though never alone.

Moss and ferns quietly soften fists;
And gently memories shift;
Memories of days of yore,
Memories of what came before.

Grandma

When I was young,
I thought of you as pure fun.
You even undertook
To teach me how to cook.
In explosions of flour, your kitchen shook;
While Grandpa hastily retired with a book.

When I was a little bolder,
I thought of you as simply older.
Set in your ways,
Critiquing my days,
As bridges, so many I burned.
Determined the world must change,
That your own life just had to re-arrange.

Now that I myself have aged,
And you are a star,
Up high and so far,
I think of you as a sage.
As I watch children of a different time,
Burning bridges, a sign
Of a different future,
Of yet another change in culture.

And as the young continue to explore

And burst out of perceived cages,
Old conventions overturned;
Furtive lessons eventually learned;
A need to stay tethered at our core;
Foundations throughout the ages,
Lasting evolutions occur in stages.

Picture You

I always picture you there,
In your chair.
On occasion, fussing with your hair;
Life's fears, tears, and joys flit across your face,
No matter the emotion, I always see grace.

Throughout the years, new lines appeared.
In the creases, your beauty in my eyes increases.
Each laugh line marked the passing of time,
A guiding compass of our shared thought mines.

Shared love, shared cares;
And I will forever picture you
In that chair
Just over there…

Dreams

Night falls and the mind decides to play.
Unfettered, toying with the events of day;
Weaving its own fantastical stories,
Fractured tales of nonsensical glories,
Pieced together,
Woven as lightly as a feather.

When logic of day,
Chases night away
And flowers open at dawn,
The mind wonders at where it has gone.
Reaching to grasp in the mist,
Its stories, ephemeral wisps.

Their meaning a quest;
Their meaning, anyone's guess,
Yet, maybe simply just this:
Shadows of thoughts unrelinquished;
A goodnight kiss, a wish;
As night falls from day,
The mind decides to play.

Lives You May Have Lived

From the depth of sleep's drift,
From the present, a boundless rift,
Reality unmoored,
Dreams in which you soared,
Exist no more.

Whenever so gently you wake,
Who you are ill-defined,
Where you are out of mind,
No idea the time of night or day,
Panic—you fight to keep at bay.
All the while, your heart pounds and shakes;
All the while, your mind scrambles and quakes.

Dangling, when time and space merge,
When who you could be and who you are converge;
No idea what century you are in,
Before the mind tumbles in,
Reveals where you have been;
And a kaleidoscope of senses
Reveals what present tense is.

Without who, where or when,
Flashes of seconds,

Past lives beckon,
With those you may have lived, contend;
Before present's veil once again descends.

A Child's Eyes

Childhood tinny speeches and screeches,
Childhood songs and wrongs,
Echoes of childhood rhymes,
Echoes of a different time.

Walk through the images,
Walk through the pages,
Of your different ages,
Echoes of different guiding sages.

Eyes glow with hope and joy,
Occasional mopes that so annoy,
Mostly, see the gleam,
Echoes of a future as yet unseen.

Now see the lines across face and brow,
Wrought by quests
For happiness
For a coherent logic
Echoes of elusive concepts.

Time and sigh blemished,
Though not diminished,
For dreams, hopes, and joy are never extinguished.
In the yearning sun,

Echoes of troubles and struggles overcome.

Images trapped in the past;
Flesh and bone touched by hour's glass;
Spirit and mind weathered to ever last;
What did the eyes of that child see?
Did she know she would become me?

In the Blood

Walk the road less traveled without a care;
Feel the wind twist and turn your hair;
Feel the warm sun rays touch your cheek;
Breathe in deep.

See the milk pods and the bulrushes in feathery bloom;
Their seedling children will be gone so soon;
Hiding remains of ragweed that always make you sneeze;
For along the creek banks, gather the weeds.

Let the emotions flood;
For the sights and scents of home,
No matter how far you roam
Are felt deep in the blood.

Walking through the mud,
Your heart gives a tug;
The scents of wood fires,
Memories conspire
In reflections steep,
Breathe in deep.

The tall grasses waving in the breeze,
Their white feather fringes you can't bear to leave.
Why do sights and scents so measly

Envelop so completely;
And bring you right back home
No matter how far you roam?
Lightning rods, so odd
Yet, they are felt deep in the blood.

Sunrises

Clouds fringed with silver and golden slivers
Incandescent, searing edges,
Warming pledges;
Open fields alight;
Far-reaching sparks
Light what was once dark.
The rise of dawn brings
Clarity to many things.

As the sun rises
And hits you right between the eyes,
Squint tight and do not let go;
Do not get lost in its glow;
For it can be easy to lose your way
In the brightest of rays.

In its continued ascent
Of rays past and present,
Clarity comes back in;
Reality burns your skin;
In the light of what is seen,
You wonder where you have been
And what you have dreamed.

Later as darkness again gathers,

And blinds what really matters,
Search and do not let go;
Do not get lost in its shifting flows.
For it can be easy to lose your way
In the darkness of day.

Yet, the very tiniest of sparks
Will always light what once was dark.

Simple Bliss

It's the moments of togetherness
Without which life would be amiss.
Simple moments;
Assuaging torments;
Smiles of complete strangers;
Complicit in joy—bridges across craters.

The times at home;
The every days, the holidays;
The love we say;
The world at bay.

The stories told
That never get old;
Sharing a kitchen
Without any friction;
How long a turkey to cook?
Complicated math,
A perilous path;
Especially when you told me it weighs six hundred pounds;
And sent me into gales of laughter,
And became a legend ever after.

The times at the buffet
When I went astray

And circled the wrong way;
The times when I followed my GPS
And you pointed out it was the other left;
The times you muttered under your breath
And God help us, I just went with yes;
The times I said it's just a short hike
And five hours later, it just didn't seem right;
The time when you shopvac'ed the mouse
That had skittered into the house;
And I asked if there were any more mice
Superhero—you replied, "In the freezer, we have ice."
The times we laughed at autocorrect
In wonder at what we would next text.

Forgiving me for being a grouch;
Falling asleep together on the couch;
Surviving arduous times;
Sharing a glass of wine;
Dogs underfoot,
All the memories time overtook.

All the simple moments of bliss
Are those in life we should never miss.

Holiday Lights

They start out slow,
Swirling around trees,
Swaying in evening's breeze;
Then as dark grows thicker,
Their patterns glitter
Across snow
Setting the most wintry hearts aglow.

More and more join in;
Swells of joy begin.
Lights bright and still
Welcomes from every window sill;
For every traveler in winter's night
Bring the child inside to light;
And the most wintry of hearts takes flight.

Le Mot Juste

Does a *"mot juste"*
Convey precision or depth?
In its presence, thrust,
In its meaning, can you trust?
Or do you need to really listen
To hear its mission?

To write it, do you want to tell?
Or with it let the reader dwell?
To write it, do you want to command,
To hold the reader in your hand?
Or do you want to let go,
To hold the reader enthralled,
In its diamond facets show?

Facets and depth;
Surreptitious meanings intercept
What is this messy brew
That explains me to you,
And you to me?
From the "brouillon" of the inner poet,
Find whatever truths inchoate.

Tell me what you see.
What is writ from the pens
From the minds that control them,
The minds of women.

Magic of the Heart

There is magic in the shape of a heart.
To understand, take it apart.

A mirror, mostly equal;
Or, in peril, any sequel;

Connected by only two rivets;
A universal symbol of love, vivid;

An inner protective divot;
Understanding, gentleness, trust within it;

No ledges;
No edges;

Just smooth swerves,
Throughout life's curves;

Yet, tapered to a fine tip;
Life's threats, to slit;

Should the heart get turned around,
Find itself upside down;

The dagger tip
Its own throat to slit;

No longer trust,
Only a deadly thrust;

Be smart,
Guard the magic of the heart.

My Strength and Stay

Someone to run problems by;
Someone to trust amid others' lies;

Someone to cast another set of eyes;
Someone to navigate difficult-to-read skies;

Someone to share life's sun and rain;
Someone who ensures no day is ever the same;

Someone who will listen to your say;
Someone who will say when you risk losing your way;

Someone who is my strength
When life gets intense.
An anchor in every storm;
A shoulder to rest on when careworn;

Someone on whom I can depend;
Someone with me 'til life's end;

Someone, as yet a dream to portray,
Someone who will be my stay.

Love Is a Verb

When Love is a noun,
It can turn a life around,
Or shut one down.
A term of endearment;
Of appeasement;
Of concealment.

When Love is a state,
All thorns it can almost escape;
All needs it can almost replace,
With equanimity and grace;
All tribulations faced,
Almost erased.

First, being named,
Then, wrapped and framed,
Now, being heard;
This is what happens, when Love is a verb.
A choice exercised;
Constantly reprised;
Never compromised.

Love is a verb.
And We exercise it.

Into Bold

Together, to grow into bold;
To salvage each other from the folds
Of what the world leaves behind.
To challenge
Never the heart
But only the mind.
To have and to hold,
To grow into old.

Time

Time moves forth in a regular way,
Or so they say.
It's a matter of science;
A matter of compliance.

Yet, life knows
There are moments when it slows;
Minutes so prolonged,
Seconds immeasurably long.

Moments of crisis and pain;
Moments after which life is never the same;
Moments in which people grow;
Moments when courage shows.

Yet, time thieves.
There are moments when it flees;
Minutes so short lived;
Seconds, immeasurably fugitive.

Moments of sheer joy aflame;
Moments after which life is never the same;
Moments in which people grow;
Moments when courage shows.

Stop Awhile

Stop awhile and gaze at the fields.
A crooked, weathered post leans,
Frames the scenes.
Just rows of mud;
Before the first buds;
Beauty yet to be revealed;
Before the crops yield.

Stop awhile and gaze at the fields.
Waist-high-fields of green;
Stretching from that little post that still leans;
A life traveler reaches out a finger;
A gentle breeze lingers;
Feel the calm, the peace triggered.

Stop awhile and gaze at the fields.
Fields of green now sky high;
Burying the little post alive;
Watching as crops bend;
As a life's traveler feels the stronger wind;
Trusting in survival through whatever life can send.

Stop awhile and gaze at the fields.
Fields of shorn and rolled gold;
That crooked little post once again seen;

And still it leans;
Stories told;
Others as yet to unfold;
Life's traveler feels peace with the past;
Renewals of wonder and awe that will last.

Stop awhile and gaze at the fields.
Fields of white unmarred;
Ever so gently hides its scars;
The little post capped with its own beret;
From whence swirls of pixie dust play;
An infinite serenity unspoken;
In their smoothness unbroken;
And in their vast light,
As winds bluster, ghosts take flight.

The One Note

The one note that pulls you in,
That's how it all begins.
The air suddenly thin;
The mind held within;
Away from thoughts of now and tomorrow;
Away from thoughts of pain and sorrow;
Longing
Belonging.

The one note that makes you soar,
That brings you to your core;
Breath halted for more;
Belonging to the score;
Away from thoughts of hurts and cares;
Away from thoughts of snares and glares;
Imploring
Restoring.

The one note that lingers,
When meaning is grasped between your fingers;
Restoration of life revealed;
The heart finally healed;
Still pining
Always shining.

No Words Needed

A tilt of your head, in face of unknowns,
When you don't understand;
When the outcome wasn't as planned;

A raised eyebrow or ear,
When thinking "crazy";
When seeing tears;

A heartfelt groan,
When asked to wake up;
When moved, snuggled up;

A repeated soft cry,
When pacing with worry;
When needing to hurry;

A softly muttered grunt,
When caught in some pretty hapless stunt;
When, at laughter, not taking affront;

A waving paw,
When attention is needed;
When your case is being pleaded;

A nibble on toes and maybe your nose,

When needing to play;
When having something to say;

A bum in the air, a tail wagging fast,
When meaning is lost in anything past;
When the present is here to last;

No words needed
For the best in life to be heeded.

Early Light

Have you ever seen anything as bright
As the early morning light?
The fog quietly hovering above the lake
As soft, pink dawn breaks.

Paddle into the Other world
As the fog unhurriedly unfurls;
Paddle into its surround
As life suspends… with hardly any sound.

Water, as calm as glass—
A peace too evanescent to last.

Hints

Throw open the window,
Stare.
Seek with the heart what the mind already knows.
Touched gently by the softest light,
The fresh, early morning air;
The hint of lilac over there;
Sweet crab-apple flowers, an exotic flare.
A glinting soft dew;
The simple promise, a day new;
The hint of possibilities.
A dare.
The hint of heat to come
Under a more merciless sun.

Not Enough

Some people find
Safety.
Living in a long straight line
Along a path.
Never a need to look back.

Why is such a life enough
For some
And not others?

Other people need
Chaos.
Living a ruckus of hills and valleys;
Sometimes, useless sallies.
Ups and downs;
Highs and lows.
They—no one—know
Where it will all go.

Why is such a life enough
For some
And not others?

Different lives lived and chosen;
Different lives survived and woven.

A chosen skin?
Frozen in?
An Omen?

Why is such a life enough
For some
And not others?

Clear choices evident;
Questions relevant;
For children to grow;
For children to know;
Met with reticence
And eloquent silence.

Why is such a life enough for some
And not others?
How do you choose what you become?
How do you not feel smothered?
When what makes one tick
Makes another's mind constrict.

Questions that can't be answered?
Knowledge that can't be transferred?

Needed

Addiction to being needed;
From life-threatening crisis to conflicts heeded;
Nectar of value, of worth;
The most alluring drug on Earth.

It all starts as a glorious flower,
One that burns with inner evil and invasive power.
'Til it changes to weed,
Feeds and feeds
On ever-encroaching inner needs.
Left unchecked,
A noose around a neck.

Left bloodied and torn,
On all its emanating thorns;
No longer able to be reformed.

Dandelions

Everyone has dandelions in their life.
Their grass rife
With encroaching spindly weeds
Sometimes, as far as eyes can see.

Weeds that will eat you alive.
Weeds that keep spreading,
Multiplying,
Leaving you crying.
Unless, addressed,
Recognized as pest,
So, you can strive.

Do you learn to see beauty in yellow?
Or simply see destruction and bellow?
Do you become complacent?
Your joy nascent,
Comforted and mellow,
When you compared yours to those of the other fellow?

Do you turn the weeds into wine?
A taste acquired over time.
Do you see symbolism everywhere?
White fluff flying through air.
Do you go on a tear?

Ripping everything, everywhere,
Not caring what is destroyed along the way;
It's the price you must pay.

Do you pull each of them out with precision?
Taking time, no matter the derision;
Knowing you can't get them all;
Knowing you will try before you fall;
A necessary cull,
Before empty platitudes lull;
For what is left,
Becomes interwoven, complex;
Festers,
Ugly splinters in your mind sequestered.

All the harms and hates;
The straggly wounds that never abate
Bloom with yellow flowers;
If not tended…
Never mended…
Overpowered…
Dreams devoured.

A Work Unfinished

Who you are frozen,
Based on past words spoken;
Based on past actions chosen.

Moments of weakness creepeth
Into every person's life;
And then judgment seepeth
Like a poison in the night.

Yet, frozen in time,
Is not truth sublime,
Rather, falsehood connived;
For experiences show
And people grow.

Backwards gaze
May be all the rage;
Look forward, take the harder task;
See change, meet the bigger ask;
No one should be diminished
When every single one of us is a work unfinished.

Winter Storm

Lower your eyes from winter's bleak and leadened skies
Beneath, the magic lies.
Every branch outlined so delicate, so fine
While heavier clumps shelter as they lay across the pines.

Each one unique when born
On gust of wind in the same direction borne.
Every now and then snow dust in mid-air lingers;
Phantom forms
Defying travel norms
Indestructible even by pointing fingers.

In this, this is where magic exists.
Courage to defy a one-directional rush;
Courage to resist;
The tumble and its shush;
The courage of dust.

No One Has a Problem with Trees

No one has a problem with diversity in trees;
Different types of trunks,
Different shapes of leaves,
Different shades of green,
Wrapped in different skins,
Yet, the same life within.

No one has a problem with diversity in trees.
If, this is indeed true,
Why should anyone have a problem with diversity in me and you?

Different trunk textures so admired,
Their quest to grow, a same fire;
Different shapes celebrated,
Their beauty consecrated;
Different desires for different reasons,
Yet, in every life, the same seasons.

Different locations and terrains,
Their sky above remains the same.

No one has a problem with diversity in trees.
If, this is indeed true
Why should anyone have a problem with diversity in me and

you?

Differences in colors and design,
Diversity in nature stirs us.
Differences in purpose and minds,
Diversity in humans disturbs us.
And is sadly too often maligned
Rather than seen as als eins.

Hidden Compartments

Walls built through the years
At first to hide fears.
Then, to hide tears.

Memories of loss,
Goodbyes at such a cost;
Empty rooms,
More than one would assume;
Hidden scars
Cast among the stars.

Walls of a maze,
Dreams just a haze;
Solid, no one ever hears the screams;
Solid, no fractures, no seams.

Dead ends.
Not one even bends;
How do you find a way home?
How do you know you are not alone?

Follow the Heart

Right and left.
To develop only one,
Leaves one
Bereft;
At whose behest?

Supplied by the heart
Of science and art.
Be both a part.

Intricately linked,
Far more than you think;
If you believe,
Science is only what you breathe,
Listen to your heart;
Follow… and there, there is Art.

Weeds of Life

How do you weed?
Do you surface clean?
'Til all is neat and gleams?
Without ever dirtying hands or feet;
Pulling those even between concrete.
Ready for others to walk at any time on your street.

Only to return in the near after
With tears and no laughter.
Realizing they never give up the fight;
And only return, not a pretty sight;
Anchored and, with so much more bite.

Or do you dig deep?
Claw to release their teeth.
'Til dirt flies,
And dust gets in your eyes;
Your arms and legs burn
To hit the point of no return.

To hit the point of belonging,
Instead of useless hope, of longing;
Hard fought; understanding wrought;
Weeds of life no longer invasive,
In the end, just order and beauty pervasive.

Roots run so far and deep;
The ground alone knows the secrets it keeps;
All the things I wish I knew.
As all things in life renew.

Power Politic

I have watched you from times of yore
Smooth talk, a gift
That concealed many a rift
A quest for power politic
In houses wherein murky clouds blow thick
Exclusivity, breath on the vine
And you climbed.

No issue you couldn't weasel 'round;
No position could pin you down.
Derided by some
Fearful of power as of a gun.

So close, so close
Watched now by crowds
As you grow ever proud
Now attained.
Will you use power to grow or constrain?
What will happen next?
Will it be hand to hand or foot to neck.

Emergence

In the near early morning light,
From a gentle unknown,
A mist of gray white,
The contours of barns,
The shapes of farms,
Come into sight.

The beauty of the present vast,
A sense of being slight,
A being lost in flight,
Of being on your own,
Entwined with the eerie unknown,
Yet, encompassed,
By the presence of the past,
And so, neither lonesome nor alone.

Within barbed wire fences.
A leaning web of past and present defenses.
Partly hidden by tall willowy grass.
A swaying soft welcome.
Yet, a stealthy warning underneath,
Such is what the country bequeaths.

Up in the Night

Up in the night,
The moon burns so bright.
Alluring, incandescence lighting your way,
While, across its face, shadows play.

Centuries of questions and still asking;
Centuries of humanity and enchantment long lasting;
In the quiet peace of the dark,
Both stars and shadows leave their mark.

Contrasts

Orange sun lights gray
As dawn chases night away.
Feel the chill touch your nose;
Feel it linger in your fingers and toes.

From the hearth,
Fires of fall elusively curl
As leaves flame and swirl;
Then fall back to Earth.

Contrasts of warm and cold;
Contrasts of gray and gold;
Feel the wonder of being alive quiver,
Before winter's crystalline whither.

Moving

Bare walls and halls,
I have wandered them all;
Now depersonalized, anonymized,
Unrecognized;
All to be conceptualized
By others;
Gone all that made them my own;
Gone all that made them home.

The moments of love and laughter
Will echo forever after.
The walls that hid the tears,
The heart stopping fears,
So that I could walk out brave;
So, who I am was always saved.

A goodbye has begun
Before the last note is even sung.
The stories a life make;
The stories no one can take;
What and how we remember
Through the embers.

Now its soul is lost and waiting;
The memories it holds slowly fading;

Wall and halls weeping;
Over the soul they will no longer be keeping.
A time of sedition;
A time of transition;
Preparing to be someone else's own.
That special place called home.

Nostalgia

Nothing is left.
Hollow echoes fall,
Pangs of heartache,
A wretch of you make.
You should have left before.
 But you had to return once more.

Up the stairs in your mind's eye.
The table was there,
The gold and black mirror above,
The painting of that girl in red,
Down the hall, she led.

The vase, the table and chair;
The bed stood right over there;
The books on the nightstand;
Titles simple and grand.
Another girl in red,
See her half turned,
Smiling in my head.

Nothing is left.
Rooms bereft;
Mind in memories sweep;
Heart in emotions weep.

It's time to say goodbye;
It's time to try not to cry;
Close the front door,
Once more.

Old Photographs

Captured smiles and poses in old photographs;
Captured moments that still make me laugh.
Look how young and thin we look
Before life's time became a crook;
Faces so full of promise and hope
Before life's moments withheld a rope.

There are pictures of those left behind,
Of names, forgotten in time;
Of places, now hard to find;
In my mind.

There are pictures of those long lost,
Of faces smiling, so soft.
Dressed in outfits of another time,
People, never hard to find,
In my mind.

Moments held hand in heart
Before life tore them apart.

Then there are pictures of those who stay
And in the fray,
Become life's rays;
Moments forgotten, now recalled,

My god, did we really live them all?

As I look and look in a daze
The past no longer cloaked in its usual haze.
I reflect on all those happy smiles
And consider the long miles.
It feels like light years have passed
Since those old photographs.

Innocent faces
Before life's hardships and graces;
Frozen in time
What kind of life was eventually mine?

Divisions

Encounters and meetings,
Always two sides to every greeting;
What is seen through whose lens,
Depends.

Easier to change interpretation
Of any given situation;
Of any given confrontation;
Than to trouble oneself
To change the self.

Across the divide,
Bitterness cannot hide.
And what is seen through whose lens,
Depends.

A narrow lens
Sees long and far;
Misses the scars for the stars
In sorrow ends.
A wider lens
Sees near and clear;
Sees the veneer ever so sheer,
And with heartache contends.

Easier to avoid vision,
Avoid revision.
Easier to change another,
And all responsibility smother
Than to trouble oneself
To change the self.

Day follows day;
Night holds sway;
And the divide grows wide;
On its tentacles hung
Bitterness stung.

In a World of No Winter
(For Lecia)

In a world of no winter,
Without harsh winds
And cracked, bleeding lips
And bitter freeze to our very tips.

In a world of long, slow spring,
With sprinkling joy and little bird twitters
And branches already fiery red at their tips
And soft, lingering breezes on our lips.

Through icy shards, spring waters gleam,
Willows gently brush the air with green
What was gone can now be seen
Yet none can wash illness clean.

Before long, you will be gone.
Before the first rose buds at dawn;
And, in a world with no winter,
Our hearts will still shiver and splinter.

Yet, in a world of no winter,
In a world of no death,
You will live fiercely in our every breath;

Our lodestar of healing, and loves true;
Of valor and finding a way through.

Know, like you
With time, we too,
Will just need a little rest.

Loss

In today's world of rhythm and rhyme,
Always, always, a wish for a little more time.

Oh, how have we arrived at this day
When there is still so much to do, so much to say,
We could have talked every hour of every day.

Caught in life's eddies and tides.
Sometimes apart, sometimes side by side;
On our own waves sometimes in valleys low, sometimes riding high;
Never guessing the end for one was nigh.

Now
Oh how…
How I lament,
Time apart, time misspent.

In today's world of rhythm and rhyme
Always, always a wish for a little time.

The Pines

Walking between rows of pines,
Stalwart, tall, in a perfect line,
A feeling of protection
Hard to define.
Branches above touching,
Hands lingering,
Friends mingling.

Their divide heavy with fallen gold unspun,
Warmed by sun,
Soft, no longer sharp,
Stark,
Yet, still in beauty spark.
A togetherness that time cannot dim,
Wander in,
Find the welcome within.

Follow the burning gold underfoot,
Away from the world that shook.
Light filtered through branches,
An invitation for taking chances;
Branches above skittering,
In the cold together shivering;
Only ever so slightly parted by storms,
As should be the norm.

And if one branch should fall,
No longer held by them all,
Tumbled to the tapestry of gold,
To repose
For the solitary traveler to find,
To remind.

Past, Present... Future?

On our way to who we have become,
Look... look at what we have done.

The Earth scorched
The lives... the dreams torched.

Those sacrificed
Lives... without a price.

The collateral harms
Hidden behind charms.

Class, skin, or thought
Are all trouble-wrought.

Any repairs
Are not ends fair.

Any us
Is not truth in which to trust.

Scars, crevices deep
Are not enough for secrets to keep.

Any light
Needs to be harsh to shine bright.

And woe is taught
By those not distraught.

On our way to what we have become
Look… look at what we have done.

Why?

Though I am generally an optimist
I never planned on a life like this.
So different it was to be
From what you now see.

Asking why
Yields no reply.
Why is there pain?
Science can provide all etiologies
Vast expanses of physiology;
Yet, ask why there is rain.
Look to the sky
Never is there a reply.

Believe in solutions
Such is my resolution.
Why is salvation denied?
Science can provide all alternatives
Vast options of confirmatives.
Yet, being alive should not be decried.
Look to the sky
Never is it too high.

Life can be derailed
Render us frail.

Why is it our spirit to defy?
Time can bring us all troubles;
Vast expanses of puddles;
Yet, happiness can be without scale.
Look to the sky
Never can it not let us fly.

Rupture

How do you say goodbye to a friend
When you part as the river bends?
When together you used to talk
Almost before you could walk.

What hurts more
The loss of sharing ideas;
Unity in front of peers;
The loss of notes compared;
Laughter shared;
The loss of shared fun;
Knowing when to run?

How did we change from what we were?
Was it because of him, of her?
Now, we no longer confer.

How is it that we now take cover?
Was it your search for power?
Now achieved, us soured.

How did we change to enmity?
Was it my quest for equality?
Now everything is weaponry.

How did we change from being soulmates?
Was it because of life's weight?
Now, everything is bait.

Say goodbye to a friend.
The river does bend.
The dream does end.
To persist
One of us would need to cease to exist.
… Separate…
How did we reach checkmate?

Oncoming Storm

In the gray anticipation
Before the winds begin to fly,
Feel the stillness of the pines;
Hear their needles drop
Across the rocks,
Waiting.

Fronts of gray marshal on;
First ice spreads across the ponds;
Almost silence, Nature's song.
And, in the still open parts,
Ripple upside down trees,
Modern Art;
Waiting.

As the sky
Emits its gray cry,
Quietly enveloping trees;
A beautiful freeze;
Waiting.

Branches now with crowns of white;
A cold new light;
A woman walks in the snow;
What is hidden…

Will now show.
Waiting.

A woman traces her path in the snow;
Studying paws;
Looking for claws;
For what was hidden…
Will now show.
Waiting.

Sheathed

Who knows what mysteries lie at hand
When fog lies across the land?
Evergreens caught in its web;
Mountains draped with trailing thread.

A sense of waiting hangs among the trees,
Undulating in the faintest breeze;
All of nature holds its breath;
And what lies beneath the sheath.

Even facades are concealed;
Only glancing truths unsealed;
Nature and humanity momentarily aligned,
As what is part of a grand design
Is far from benign.

Rather, it's not so subtle threat,
Hides what could happen next;
Answers never to be found,
In any school child's text.

After the Rain

Skies different hues of gray,
Untouched still by the sun's rays,
Suspended in mid-air,
So nearly not there,
Phantom wisps ever so slowly drift,
Majestically changing shapes in the mist.

Haunting mountain emerald greens,
Completely changing scenes.
A sense of time standing still;
A thought of dreams yet to fulfill.

Yet, skies too soon clear;
Haunting mists disappear;
And whispering zephyrs of lace
Vanish, without a trace.

Blaze of Glory

As you walk in the fading light,
Past quiet river edges and ponds,
Rimmed with the softest of green fronds,
Hear the birds and frogs sing with all their might,
In the still, clear spring night.

New, bright colors slowly muted,
As dusk descends undisputed;
Here, earth and sky separate;
The blaze of glory refuses to abate;
Startling reds intense against graying clouds,
Defying all attempts to shroud.

Undaunted, refusing to bow,
A near human will, here and now;
And, as red fades to pink,
A last refusal to sink.

After Dark

Even though in the light of day,
You admire nature in all its ways;
Night is a different thing;
Winds of haunted rustlings,
Hearts stop in nature trusting.

A foreign land
Is at hand;
Do you dare go outside?
What does the dark now hide?

How strange the world has become
After the setting of the sun;
Dark creeps all around;
What was that? A sound?
Who is there? Ghosts abound
Eyes shine in the dark
Over there—deep in the park.

A foreign land
Is at hand;
Do you dare go outside?
What does the dark now hide?

Fall

Air with a certain crispness,
Wind with a certain briskness,
Before the calendar announces any change at all,
The morning air reveals the arrival of fall.

A time of unstoppable change, a prediction;
Do you feel a tenseness, a superstition?
As the air sharpens your awareness,
Can you feel your pulse quicken?
At what remains unwritten?

Corner Bookstore

As you walk through the door
Of the corner bookstore,
See the shiny new titles gleam;
See the Old Masters' classics stately sheen;
Fingers brush across bindings;
Yearnings, quests, findings.

For love, for equity, for justice fights;
The quests of all human knights.
Thoughts, ideas, philosophical forays;
The results of all human laboratories.
Through the centuries
Thread the stories.

What has been gained?
Why are our struggles still in the same vein?
What has been changed?
What has been re-invented?
What has been prevented?
Where are we now in the present?

In the corner bookstore,
See what has been before;
See what can't be seen online;
Find
The threads of us.
Discuss.

Before You Roam

Know your own home
Before you roam.
From coasts of sandy beaches,
The subject of too many speeches,
To spectacular rocky shoreline,
From whence the sun begins to shine,
Crashing waves smashing their own redesign.

Understand all your peoples' history,
Cultures and sense of mystery,
Tall tales of the sea,
Real tales of bravery,
Moments of creativity,
Moments of sheer treachery.

Cultivate a spirit of inquisitivity.
Learn to celebrate diversity.
Try as hard as you can
To be able to understand
Those from a different land.

From the mountains on either end,
From wherever the river bends,
In every tree and stone,
Understand the lands that own
Understand before you roam.

Be Careful Going the Rest of the Way

As day succeeds day,
Throughout my ages,
As storms rage,
Falling rain darkens day's light,
With you, I share my choices,
To stand and fight;
My choices
To take flight.

Winter storms diamond sparkle,
Their rages marvel;
And, driving snow lights
The darkness of nights.
With you, I share
The slights and plights,
And all my frights.

And as time screeches toward our midnight,
You are my searchlight
For what I should have done in hindsight;
My anxieties somewhat allayed,
By the love you always convey.

In the darkness, I always smile;
Across the separating miles,
When I hear you say,
Be careful going the rest of the way.

As year succeeds year,
Creeping age wreaks havoc on all those held dear;
Rivulets of tears,
Unspoken fears,
And far, far too soon,
It's my turn to say
Be careful going the rest of the way.

Joy

Most lives are too filled with daily strains
Struggles and mundane pains
Travels through forests
Dappled with moments of happiness
Eclipsed by others' clouds of pettiness.

Every now and then
Above the noise and endless din
A breath is caught
Sun through the battles fought
Something oh so precious begins.

Shared with others
Nothing can eclipse
The Arc of life on its ellipse
Through foibles and ploys
Sheer unadulterated joy.

When all crisis is over and done
And quiet peace found in ribbons of setting sun.

No greater memory should remain
Than that carved over and over;
In endless refrains;
The sharing of joy.

What I Wish I Had Known…

Make mistakes.
Risks are yours to take.
There is seldom one perfect shot.
Life is a messy, beautiful onslaught.
Don't always do as you are aught.

Don't dwell on "What If?"
So many regrets as it is.
An endless list
By the time you will read this.

Know you are tough
Or at least strong enough.
To get through most days
And as for the others,
Resilience you will uncover.

Look for what you can discover.
Don't hide under or within covers.
Use your own mind.
Life holds wondrous finds.
You may be maligned,
Who cares? Don't be confined.

Do not be afraid of commitment.

Fight indifference.
In the ink of a pen,
Change can be written.

Capture dreams before thy alight.
Chase storms before they take flight.
Life is the Aurora Borealis in a darkest night.
In incandescent swirls,
In phantasmic curves and twirls,
Glowing a beauty of unnatural green.
Glowing a beauty rare and largely unseen.

New Beginnings

An irrevocable decision made;
A final price paid.

A fateful turn of page;
The end of the craze.

The secret still mine;
Alone;
Owned at this moment in time.

A chapter hard fought;
A peace lost sought.

Over in a life's blink;
Deep in forested links.

A goodbye before the abyss;
Time always to reminisce.

Memories buried deep in mind;
Stories yet to find.

Nothing to atone;
A step into the unknown.

A new beginning, a seed sown;
New dreams… all my own.

Every Night

Every night,
In the dimming light,
I point my feet toward home
With such relief;
Days full of toil and trouble,
Dreams reduced to rubble,
Life's sheaf;
Boundless grief.

Every night,
In the dimming light,
I point my feet toward home
With such anger;
Days full of hope and yearning,
Dreams lost and burning,
Life's render,
Smouldering surrender.

Every night,
In the dimming light,
I point my feet toward home
With such longing;
Days full of moments awry,
Dreams reduced to tears and cries,
Life's sting,

Forget belonging.

Every night,
In the dimming light,
I point my feet toward home
With such exhaustion;
Days full of thorns and worn,
Dreams scattered and torn,
Life's omen,
Endless ocean.

Every night,
In the dimming light,
I point my feet toward home
With such gratitude;
Days survived,
Dreams modified,
Still alive;
Life's étude,
A quiet triumph accrued.